KU-130-344

Contents

WITHDRAWN FROM BROMLEY LIBRA

Beyond the Great Wall

For centuries, people have risked life and limb to cross stormy seas, deadly jungles and barren deserts in search of new lands to conquer and places to trade. But few have travelled further than thirteenth-century globetrotter Marco Polo.

In 1271, 17-year-old Marco Polo set off from his home in Venice, Italy, on a journey across Asia to the court of Kublai Khan, the Chinese Emperor. With his father and uncle, Marco travelled across Persia (modern Iran) through wild, mountainous country. Attacked by bandits, the three merchants fled for safety to a nearby castle. Hoping to travel by sea, they headed for the Persian Gulf. But Marco was horrified at the local ships, describing them as 'the worst I've ever seen!'

△ Built to protect the northern border of the mighty Khan's empire, the 8,851 kilometre-long Great Wall of China is one of many marvels Marco Polo saw during his travels.

Daring Journeys

Jim Pipe

Bromley Libraries

30128 80170 325 0

First published in 2014 by Franklin Watts

Copyright © Franklin Watts 2014

Franklin Watts
338 Euston Road
London NW1 3BH

Franklin Watts Australia
Level 17/207 Kent Street
Sydney, NSW 2000

All rights reserved.

Produced for Franklin Watts by White-Thomson Publishing Ltd

www.wtpub.co.uk
+44 (0) 843 208 7460

Edited and designed by Paul Manning

A CIP catalogue record for this book is available from the British Library.

Dewey no: 904
Hardback ISBN: 978 1 4451 3423 9
Library eBook ISBN: 978 1 4451 3649 3

Printed in China

Franklin Watts is a division of Hachette Children's Books,
an Hachette UK company.
www.hachette.co.uk

Picture credits:
Front cover, Shutterstock/Praseodimio; 3, 5, Getty/Gordon Wiltsie; 6, Shutterstock/James
Stuart Griffith; 7, Shutterstock/Fan Ping; 8, 9b, Tim Severin; 10b, Shutterstock/Pichugin
Dmitry; 11, Getty/Hulton; 12t, 12b, Sarah Outen; 13, Jude Edginton; 14, Shutterstock/Igor
Plotnikov; 15, Corbis/Didrik Johnck; 16 (background), Shutterstock/Leksele; 16t, 16b, Ramon
Larramendi; 18 (background), Shutterstock/Ronen; 18t, Shutterstock/Kjersti Joergensen;
19, Steve Backshall; 20, Dave Cornthwaite; 21, Shutterstock/Robert Paul Van Beets;
22 Corbis/George Steinmetz; 22t, Corbis/Narendra Shrestha; 24, Airport Journals; 25,
Getty Images News; 26, (background) Shutterstock/Annetje; 26, National Geographic/
Getty Images.

Every attempt has been made to clear copyright. Should there be any inadvertent
omission please apply to the publisher for rectification.

Hey there! Before reading this book, it's really important for you to know
that the activities shown in it are meant for you to enjoy reading and for no
other purpose. The activities depicted are really dangerous; trying to do them
could hurt or even kill you. They should only be done by professionals who
have had a lot of training and, even then, they are still really dangerous and
can cause injury. So we don't encourage you to try any of these activities.
Just enjoy the read!

Continuing their journey on land, the Polos crossed the mountainous 'roof of the world' in Central Asia, an area bristling with fierce tribesmen 'dressed in skins of beasts'. After a year in Tibet, the Polos trekked across the Lop Nur and Gobi deserts. Here, Marco heard strange voices that could 'lure a traveller away from the path so that he never finds it again'.

The Forbidden City

After three years on the road, the Polos finally reached China. Marco was amazed by what he saw, especially the Khan's giant palace at Khanbalig (now Beijing). Known as the 'Forbidden City', the palace had rooms decorated with golden dragons, paintings of battles and countless statues of warriors, birds and animals.

When the Polos eventually headed for home 17 years later, the Khan gave them a fleet of 14 giant junks. After braving shipwrecks, disease and pirates, they finally made it back to Venice in 1295, scruffy and exhausted, but laden with jewels!

A TRAVELLER'S TALES

In 1298, Marco Polo spent a year in prison, where he dictated the story of his incredible journeys to a fellow prisoner. He described the marvels he had seen, such as coal, paper money and asbestos, and also included some unlikely tales about cannibals, men with tails, dragons, unicorns and other strange monsters. The book became a medieval bestseller, and has captured the imagination of readers ever since.

▼ The vast complex of palaces known as the 'Forbidden City' was the home of the Chinese emperor and his household for more than 500 years.

The Sindbad Voyage

The adventures of Sindbad the Sailor are among the most famous seafaring yarns of all time. But could they have been based on fact?

In November 1980, British writer and adventurer Tim Severin set out on a voyage with a difference. He planned to sail from Muscat, Oman, to Guangzhou in China, to prove that Sindbad's amazing voyages could really have taken place.

▲ Severin's ship was an exact replica of a ninth-century Arab sailing vessel. Raising the mainsail was a massive task that took at least eight men.

During the voyage Severin insisted on using only the equipment that would have been available at the time. His ship, the *Sohar*, was specially made from timbers lashed together with coconut rope. Food was basic, and there were no modern navigational instruments or radio on board to call for help if the ship got into difficulties.

Sea monsters

Fortunately, Severin and his crew didn't have to cope with one-eyed giants or the huge sea monsters that plagued Sindbad's voyages. But they did face other hazards. Rats scuttled around in the bilges, mice raided the food lockers, and a plague of cockroaches crawled over their faces at night.

Becalmed

On several occasions, the *Sohar* was nearly crushed by oil tankers; strong winds snapped the mainsail spar in two; and for almost a month, the ship was becalmed. The crew only survived by learning how to catch sharks for food and funnel rainwater into buckets. There was also the risk of attack by local pirates, not to mention huge tropical storms.

Journey's end

Finally, the ship reached the mouth of the Pearl River, before sailing triumphantly up to Guangzhou for an official welcome worthy of Sinbad himself. In all, the voyage took nearly eight months.

▼ Severin and his crew inspect the jagged stump of their broken mainsail spar. After the damage was repaired, the ship went on to complete the voyage in excellent condition.

MAN OR MYTH?

Could Sindbad the Sailor have been a real person? Severin believed so: 'The Sindbad storytellers took one captain and added other adventures to his own.' In the process, the historical Sindbad gradually turned from man into myth.

To the Heart of Africa

Even with a support team of 4x4 jeeps and the best equipment money can buy, journeying through central Africa today is full of dangers. But imagine the perils faced by the great nineteenth-century explorers like David Livingstone....

⬥ In 1855, Scottish explorer and missionary David Livingstone became the first European to discover the Victoria Falls on the Zambezi River. He later wrote: 'No one can imagine the beauty of the view from anything seen in England.'

'The lion shook Livingstone "like a terrier does a rat".'

In 1855, when Scottish missionary David Livingstone crossed Africa from coast to coast, there were no maps or mobile phones and most of sub-Saharan Africa was uncharted. First aid was basic, and the local tribespeople were often very suspicious of foreigners.

'Dr Livingstone, I presume?'

In 1871, no one had heard any news from Livingstone for three years, so US reporter Henry Stanley went to search for him. Finally tracking him down at Ujiji on Lake Tanganyika, Stanley put out his hand and said the famous words, 'Dr Livingstone, I presume?'

Animal attack

It's no wonder people thought Livingstone might be dead. While travelling more than 2,000 kilometres through the jungle, Livingstone had suffered 31 doses of fever, been attacked by huge swarms of fierce mosquitoes and had his flimsy canoe tipped over by a hippo (still Africa's deadliest killer).

A few years before, Livingstone had almost been killed by a lion that grabbed him by the arm and shook him 'like a terrier does a rat'. Livingstone had eleven tooth marks as permanent scars and the bone at the top of his left arm was crunched into splinters.

EXPLORING THEN AND NOW

The clothes Victorian explorers wore seem ridiculously impractical today: Mary Kingsley (1862-1900) climbed Mount Cameroon in West Africa in ankle-length leather boots, carrying an umbrella to shield herself from the blazing sun. When she fell into an animal trap with long spikes, she said, 'It is at these moments that you realise the blessings of a good thick skirt!'

◄ In Victorian times, explorers like Livingstone spent long periods out of contact with the outside world, often facing hair-raising dangers and hardships.

Across the Big Blue

By the end of the last century, most of the Earth's surface had been explored – but people are still looking for impossible challenges. In 2009, Sarah Outen, nicknamed 'Sarah the Stubborn' by her fans, spent over 124 days at sea battling high winds and giant waves in a successful bid to row the Indian Ocean – alone!

◀ At the age of 24, Sarah Outen was ready for a challenge. What better than rowing from Australia to Mauritius in an open boat?

▲ Solo ocean-rowing is as much about determination as physical stamina. Says Sarah: 'If you're mentally strong and well prepared psychologically, you'll have the best chance – be stubborn and strong, and with luck you'll weather the worst of the storms.'

'Be stubborn and strong, and with luck you'll weather the worst of the storms'

Sarah Outen set out in her six-metre-long rowing boat *Serendipity* (nickname 'Dippers') from Western Australia on 1 April 2009. Raging storms often made it impossible to steer or row, and Sarah was trapped inside the tiny cabin for days on end. Being tossed around like a pea in a tin can made her horribly seasick. Bad weather and ocean currents also added an extra 1,800 kilometres to her journey.

Epic journey

Sarah had trained long and hard for her epic journey, in the gym, on bikes, running marathons and out at sea. A team of experts taught her sea survival and navigation skills. But no amount of training can prepare you for the dangers of the open ocean. Sarah had to avoid being crushed by giant container ships; she also braved encounters with whales.

A final obstacle

Sarah was nearing the islands of Mauritius at the end of her journey when disaster struck. As she tried to row through a narrow gap in the coral reef, a huge wave caught her boat and capsized it, throwing Sarah into the sea. She struggled back into the boat and completed the journey unaided. She later said, 'Having rowed all this way, I wasn't about to ask for a rescue when I was just 300 metres from the entrance to the bay!' Aged just 24, she was the youngest woman to ever row across an ocean solo.

▼ *By the end of her journey, Sarah had covered almost 5,750 kilometres of open ocean. Despite eating 500 bars of chocolate, she lost 20 kilos in weight from the effort of rowing.*

SHARK ATTACK

Tough as it was, Sarah's trip could have been a lot worse. In 2005, a transatlantic rowing team were attacked by a huge shark: the four-metre-long killer hurled itself repeatedly against the hull of the small craft. During the same race, another boat sank and two other rowers were swept overboard, though luckily no lives were lost.

Into the Death Zone

Would you like to climb the world's highest mountain? Be warned: Everest has claimed at least 240 lives, including eight who perished during a 1996 storm high on the mountain. Conditions near the summit are brutal: many corpses have been left where they fell, and some can still be seen, preserved forever in the snow and ice.

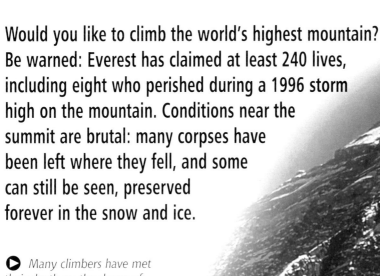

▶ *Many climbers have met their death on the slopes of Everest. The area above 7,800 metres is known as the 'Death Zone' because the lack of oxygen there can be fatal.*

WITHOUT OXYGEN

In 1978, Italian Reinhold Messner and Austrian Peter Habeler broke all the rules by reaching the top of Everest – without oxygen. Messner later described how he felt as if his 'lungs were going to burst' and his mind seemed to 'go dead'. Two years later, he reached the summit on his own without a support team, ladders or oxygen – the first, and so far the only, person ever to have done this.

> 'Lack of oxygen makes you sick and dizzy. It can also play tricks on your mind.'

Since Sir Edmund Hillary and Sherpa Tenzing Norgay made the first successful attempt on Everest in 1953, many other climbers have beaten a path to the summit. But climbing the world's highest mountain remains a supreme test of skill and endurance.

Danger 1 – Bits start falling off

Frostbite is one of the most common dangers. When your body freezes, the skin becomes black and swollen. In bad cases, fingers, ears, noses, cheeks and toes simply fall off.

Danger 2 – Sun damage

Wear dark goggles or sunglasses. Snowblindness, caused by looking at bright white snow for too long, can seriously damage your eyes.

Danger 3 – Freezing to death

If your body temperature drops below 32°C you can die of hypothermia in just 30 minutes. The best protection is to wear lots of layers.

Danger 4 – Dizzy heights

Lack of oxygen makes you sick and dizzy. It can also play tricks on your mind and even cause hallucinations.

Danger 5 – Blasted by wind and snow

The weather can change dramatically in just a few minutes at the top of a mountain. In 1996, hurricane-force winds on the top of Everest killed eight people in a single day.

Danger 6 – Avalanche

Avalanches are a constant threat, when giant slabs of snow thunder down the mountainside. They can be set off by loud noises, so avoid yelling to other climbers!

▶ *Despite the dangers, Everest still attracts men and women eager to test themselves to the limit. In May 2001, American Erik Weihenmayer (right) became the first blind mountaineer to reach the summit.*

To the Ends of the Earth

In 2005-6, a Spanish team became the first expedition ever to cross the Antarctic using wind-powered sleds. They also set the record for the longest distance travelled in one day across the Antarctic ice – 311 kilometres. These extracts from the team's diary give an idea of the challenges they faced.

◬ Using kite-drawn sleds, the Spanish team crossed the Antarctic in record time, skimming across the ice at speeds of up to 64 kph.

25 December 2005

The team spend Christmas in Vostok in the middle of Antarctica, officially the coldest place on Earth, with -89°C recorded in 1983. The whole base is 'buried under the snow, so you have to go in through a snow tunnel.' Afterwards they return to their tent, where the temperature is a bone-numbing -30°C.

▶ The Spanish Antarctic team (left to right): Juan Manuel Viu, team leader Ramón Larramendi and Ignacio Oficialdegui.

28 December 2005

Even though they're making good progress, all three men are shattered after covering 191 kilometres in just 12 hours. There are still 1,500 kilometres to go and they're worried about what lies ahead – 'the terrain is just so unpredictable'.

4 January 2006

No wind to blow their kites means the sleds have slowed right down. While most expeditions worry about blizzards, for Larramendi and his team, lack of wind spells disaster.

8–9 January 2006

The return of very strong winds, now blowing at over 50 kph, brings fresh problems. Several times the team are forced to switch to smaller kites, a job that can take an hour and a half. Meanwhile, icy ridges on the snow, known as *sastrugi*, are causing damage to the sleds.

▼ *Antarctica is Earth's southernmost continent. About 98 per cent of it is covered by ice and only the hardiest plants and animals survive.*

11 January 2006

Disaster! The team get lost during a snowstorm. 'We wanted to arrive at the meeting point with the helicopter and we were actually almost falling asleep. We were carrying several bags wrapped in cloth which broke, so we lost our satellite phone, food – even the saucepan we used to melt snow!' Amazingly, after a couple of hours of frantic searching, all the lost equipment is recovered.

13 January 2006

The three adventurers finally make it across the frozen continent in record time. Larramendi is delighted: 'We made it – it is fabulous!'

THE DEADLY POLES

In any polar expedition, the weather can mean the difference between life and death. In October 1911, two rival expeditions set off in a race to the South Pole. Norwegian Roald Amundsen's party used skis and dog sleds. Moving quickly across the ice, they reached the South Pole on 14 December. English explorer Robert Scott arrived a month later. Already worn out from dragging heavy loads across the ice, two of his men died in terrible blizzards. Scott and two others froze to death.

The Lost World

Deep in the heart of the Pacific island of Borneo is a lost world of mountains, jungles and plunging ravines whose unique wildlife is disappearing fast. In 2007, a team of scientists including naturalist and TV presenter Steve Backshall trekked into this wilderness to film the amazing animals that live there, including some that had never been seen before…

For two days, the team hauled heavily-laden canoes through the rainforest, when suddenly a tropical storm erupted overhead and the stream they were following turned into a raging torrent. Before they knew it, one of the canoes was smashed against the rocks – and, in Steve Backshall's words, 'all hell broke loose'.

◀ Borneo's gibbons are an endangered species. The main threat to their survival is habitat loss, but many are also caught by poachers to be sold as pets.

'At night, giant poisonous centipedes scuttled around the cave walls'

Caves of the dead

Eventually the crew made it to Imbak Canyon. At night, they slept in hammocks above the ground to avoid being attacked by wild animals. Steve waited for four days and nights in an ancient burial ground to try and film a huge python. It was pretty creepy hanging out in vine-entangled caves surrounded by 350-year-old wooden coffins.

▼ *The jungle is a tough place to travel – hot, sweaty and crawling with bugs. Leeches have to be picked off the body constantly, and tropical storms can bring rainforest trees crashing down without warning.*

Centipedes

Later, the team spent three nights camped on the floor of a 300-metre-deep cave. Not that they got much sleep: at night, giant poisonous centipedes scuttled around the cave walls at high speed, and huge crickets invaded their camp.

At the other end of the canyon, camerawoman Justine Evans built a tree platform and waited several days before finally being able to film gibbons swinging through the jungle canopy. With incredible sights like these captured on film, the jungle journey was worth all the hardship and danger.

▼ *TV presenter Steve Backshall has made many journeys to remote regions of the world in search of rare and unusual animals.*

WARNING: HEADHUNTERS!

In the past, remote parts of Borneo were populated by fierce tribes who were notorious for beheading and eating the flesh of their enemies. Headhunting – the traditional practice of removing a person's head after killing them – died out long ago in Borneo. However, visitors to isolated villages can still come across ancient dried skulls (once believed by locals to be a source of powerful magic).

Across the Never-Never

Known as the outback, or 'Never-Never', Australia's vast interior is one of the most forbidding places on Earth. In the daytime, think Death Valley or the Sahara. At night, think dingoes, snakes, poisonous spiders and scorpions. Now imagine making a five-month trip across 5,823 kilometres of it – on a skateboard!

People said he was mad. Privately, he agreed. But by the time 26-year-old former graphic designer Dave Cornthwaite *(right)* set off from Perth in August 2007 to cross the Australian outback on a skateboard, there was no turning back.

From the outset of his epic trip from Perth to Brisbane, Dave was determined to make it work. 'I wanted to show that if you are stuck in a rut... you don't have to stay there. You only live once.'

► *Welsh-born Dave had been skateboarding for just a year before setting out on his Australian adventure. In 2006, he set a record by skateboarding the length of Britain in just 34 days. The marathon Australian trip was his second challenge.*

Empty desert

The harsh realities of travelling day after day in blistering heat soon hit home. In the Great Dividing Range, the hills were steep. On the downhill stretches the only way Dave could brake was by dragging his foot along the ground. During his journey he wore out 14 pairs of shoes and five sets of skateboard wheels.

Injury

Amazingly, the only serious injury Dave suffered was in Adelaide: while filming an interview for local TV, he injured his heel and had to spend the next ten days on crutches. He also got a nasty bump when he flew off his skateboard at 40 kph on the final leg of his journey into Brisbane – if he hadn't been wearing his helmet, it would have been a lot worse.

By the end, Dave's right thigh was three inches thicker than his left. But he maintains that anyone can do what he did if they are determined. 'I didn't eat the diet of an elite athlete. I wanted to show that any normal person could do this.'

NO TREES

Stretching 3,900 kilometres – nearly as far as from London to Moscow – Australia's Nullarbor (literally, 'no tree') Plain boasts the longest straight stretch of road in the world. It's also the world's largest single slab of rock. To make up for the lack of landscape features, travellers can expect to see varied wildlife, from bouncing kangaroos and shingleback lizards to wedge-tailed eagles.

Traffic wasn't a problem during this section of Dave's trip.

Atlantis of the Sands

Sir Ranulph Fiennes is the world's greatest living explorer. He has led more than 30 expeditions, including the first solo crossing of the Antarctic continent and a mission to discover the lost city of Ubar in the Omani desert.

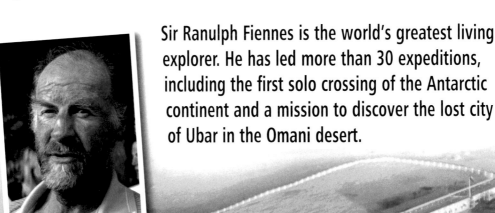

🔺 According to legend, Ubar in the Omani Desert was once a fabulously wealthy trading centre. It was built on top of a large cavern. When this collapsed around 2,500 years ago, it destroyed the oasis that provided the city's water. After Ubar was abandoned, the city gradually became buried under the sand.

SANDSTORMS AND VIPERS

In the early 1990s, after eight failed attempts, Ranulph Fiennes became the first to find the lost city of Ubar in the Omani desert (called 'the Atlantis of the Sands' by Lawrence of Arabia). His team had to overcome sandstorms and deadly vipers to locate the city's stone walls and mud-brick towers.

Not all of Fiennes' expeditions met with success. In February 2000 his attempt to become the first person to reach the true North Pole without a support team ended in failure. One week into what should have been a 1,100-kilometre journey, Sir Ranulph tried to rescue a pair of sledges that had fallen through the ice. He suffered severe frostbite as a result and lost the tips of all the fingers on his left hand.

What made you want to be an explorer?

'Well, I took it up in the first place in order to make a living after leaving the army. I didn't want to become an adventure training instructor, so leading expeditions seemed to be the only way of doing it.'

Which of your expeditions was the most dangerous?

'The one that frightened me the most only actually lasted five days – that was climbing the north face of the Eiger mountain. It amazed me that I actually made it to the top without dying of fright on the way up.'

Is there anything you always take with you on your adventures?

'Well, being a wimp, I always take this special cream. Whenever I get bitten by bugs or stung by nettles, I put this stuff on and it stops all itches immediately.'

Who are your heroes?

'There's a guy called Wilfred Thesiger, a great desert traveller, particularly in the 1950s. In terms of polar travel, Sir Wally Herbert is the best polar explorer that I know.' [*Herbert is best known for leading the 1968-9 expedition to cross the frozen surface of the Arctic Ocean, a journey of more than 6,000 kilometres.*]

Chasing the Wind

Daredevil explorer Steve Fossett was brave, stubborn and determined. Although he was already a record-breaking sailor and aviator, it took him ten years of hard work to prepare for his solo round-the-world voyage in a hot air balloon.

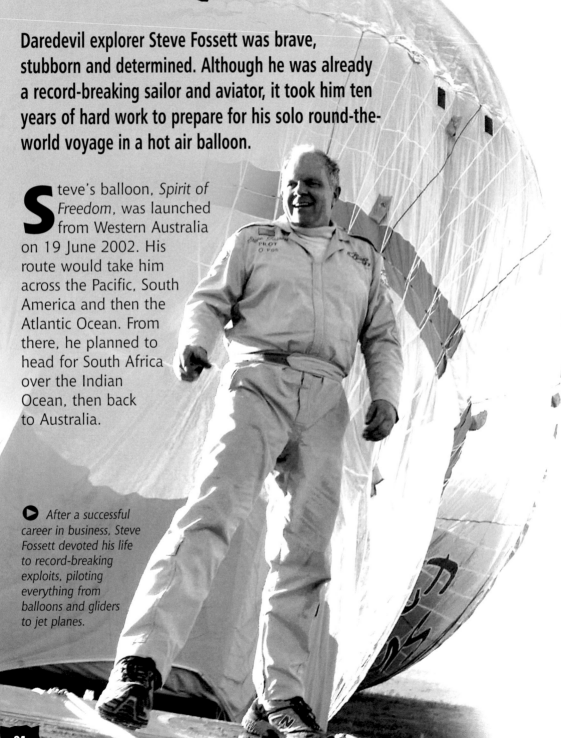

Steve's balloon, *Spirit of Freedom*, was launched from Western Australia on 19 June 2002. His route would take him across the Pacific, South America and then the Atlantic Ocean. From there, he planned to head for South Africa over the Indian Ocean, then back to Australia.

▶ *After a successful career in business, Steve Fossett devoted his life to record-breaking exploits, piloting everything from balloons and gliders to jet planes.*

Dicing with danger

Steve knew the dangers – in 1998, his balloon had plummeted 8,000 metres into the sea and he had had to wait 72 hours before being rescued. In another attempt, the balloon flew straight into a vicious thunderstorm and Steve used up so much fuel that he ended up drifting into the Andes mountains.

Thrills and spills

Eventually, Steve made it in around 15 days – but only just! At one point he had to fly incredibly low to avoid high winds. The day before he landed, one of the gas tanks caught fire. Luckily, he was awake and dived for the shut-off valves just in time. When the balloon landed in Australia, it dragged along the ground for 20 minutes, and only Steve's cabin survived.

Was it worth it? Yes, Steve was ecstatic when he landed. He'd already tried and failed five times. But he refused to give up. This time, he'd made it all the way round.

STEVE FOSSETT, 1944–2007

In an extraordinary life, Fossett set 116 world records. As well as making the first non-stop solo flight around the world in a single-engine jet aircraft, he also set cross-country skiing records, swam the English Channel and climbed the highest peaks on six continents. In September 2007, Steve Fossett's plane disappeared over the Nevada desert. The crash site was later discovered by a hiker.

⬥ *Fossett's balloon, Spirit of Freedom was as high as a ten-storey building, but the cabin he occupied was tiny. To survive at altitude, he had to wear warm clothes and breathe from an oxygen mask. He often had to climb outside the cabin in the freezing cold to check the burners and the fuel supply.*

Deep Sea Mission

At the bottom of the ocean is a world as hostile and strange as any distant planet. The weight of the water alone is deadly: 10,000 metres below the surface, the pressure is a thousand times greater than at the surface – enough to crush a regular submarine like a tin can.

The only vessels capable of surviving the harsh conditions in this alien world are deep-sea submersibles. Perhaps the most famous is *Alvin*, named after its inventor, oceanographer Allyn Vine. In the last 45 years, *Alvin* has carried more than 12,000 people down to the ocean floor.

▼ *Designed to dive to depths of up to 4,500 metres,* Alvin *is fitted with robotic arms to pick up rock samples and other objects from the ocean bed.*

Bomb disposal

Two years after it was launched, *Alvin* was used to recover an atomic bomb. The deadly weapon had been lost in the sea off the coast of Spain after a mid-air collision between a US bomber and a tanker aircraft. If it had exploded or fallen into the wrong hands, the consequences could have been devastating.

A year later, *Alvin* was attacked by a swordfish, which got caught up in the sub's equipment. The fish was dragged back to the surface with *Alvin* and cooked for dinner!

A lucky escape

During one launch, *Alvin*'s support cables failed and the vessel sank in 1,500 metres of water. The pilot escaped, but the vessel remained on the bottom until the following year. Lunches left on board were found to be soggy but surprisingly fresh, thanks to near-freezing temperatures and the lack of oxygen at the bottom!

'Black smokers'

In 1977, scientists used *Alvin* to discover amazing thermal vents known as 'black smokers' on the Pacific Ocean floor near the Galápagos Islands. Over the past 30 years it has collected all sorts of deep-sea wildlife using its robotic arms. Who knows what else lurks in the deepest parts of the oceans – there's so much still to explore!

FIRST TO THE OCEAN FLOOR

On 23 January 1960, Swiss oceanographers Jacques Piccard (top) and Don Walsh (bottom) reached the deepest point in the Earth's surface, the Challenger Deep in the western North Pacific, diving to a depth of 10,916 metres in the bathyscaphe Trieste. The descent took almost five hours, and the two men spent barely 20 minutes on the ocean floor before starting the long journey back to the surface. Fifty years later, they are still the only people to have reached this depth.

How Daring Are You?

1 A friend has asked you to join him on a transatlantic sailing trip. Would you:
   a Take a fishing line and hope to catch enough fish to survive?
   b Stock up with rations to last you, even if the voyage takes longer than expected?
   c Insist on a support vessel with its own chef and a larder full of goodies?

2 What's your idea of a challenging expedition?
   a Crossing a desert with nothing more than a tube of sunblock and a wide-brimmed hat?
   b Climbing a mountain with an experienced team after months of planning?
   c Popping to the local takeaway with an order for ten friends?

3 You're wading waist-deep through a mangrove swamp when you come face to face with a crocodile. Would you:
   a Leap on top of it and try and wrestle it into submission?
   b Wade slowly and carefully past, keeping a close eye on its movements?
   c Pinch yourself very hard in the hope that any second you will wake up from this nightmare; then turn over and snuggle back under the duvet?

4 You're rafting down a river when you see foaming white water ahead. Would you:
   a Paddle like a maniac, shouting, 'Last one to shoot the rapids is a wimp!'
   b Paddle to the bank and see if there is a way to carry the raft past the rapids?
   b Regret not having stayed in your hotel and gone for the hot tub experience instead?

5 What would you always take with you on an expedition?
   a A huge rifle with telescopic sights for hunting big game?
   b A map and compass, a good supply of water, a box of matches for lighting fires and a powerful torch to help you find your way in the dark?
   c A good selection of DVDs to watch in the back of your deluxe camper van?

Check your score

Mostly a's You're a hardcore adventurer – but you might not survive very long in the wild!

Mostly b's You're adventurous without taking stupid risks – the right sort of person to take on an expedition.

Mostly c's Sounds like you probably don't want to stray too far. Why not watch a travel show from the comfort of your sofa?

Glossary

altitude height above sea level

asbestos a type of material once mixed with cement and used for building

avalanche a landslide of snow, ice or rocks

aviator a pilot or flyer

bathyscaphe a type of manned **submersible**

becalmed (of a sailing boat) unable to move due to lack of wind

bilge the lowest part of a boat or ship

blizzard a violent snowstorm

cannibal person who eats the flesh of another human being

centipede a worm-like creature with many small legs

coral reef a rock-like mass made up of tiny sea creatures

cricket a type of grasshopper-like insect

daredevil a person who enjoys risky sports and activities

dingo a wild dog found in Australia

endurance the ability to keep going

exploit a daring feat

frostbite a painful skin condition caused by extreme cold

gibbon a species of ape found in tropical and sub-tropical jungles

glider a light aircraft that rides on currents of warm air

globetrotter a person who travels all over the world

hammock a bed hung above the ground

hypothermia life-threatening condition caused by exposure to extreme cold

junk a Chinese sailing ship

leech a blood-sucking slug-like creature

mainsail the largest sail on a boat or ship

oceanographer scientist who studies the world's oceans

outback the remote inland or desert areas of Australia

python a type of snake that is not poisonous but throttles its prey

ravine a steep-sided rocky gorge

robotic remote-controlled

scorpion poisonous insect found in hot countries

sled(ge) a vehicle with runners for travelling across snow or ice

spar a length of timber used as a mast or to support a sail

stubborn determined not to give up or change one's point of view

submersible a type of vessel designed for deep-sea diving

summit the highest point of a mountain

valve a device for controlling the flow of liquids or gases

viper a poisonous snake

Websites

www.nationalgeographic.com
Great photos, background information and real-life adventure stories.

http://solarsystem.nasa.gov/index.cfm
Find out about NASA's plans to explore our solar system.

http://www.survivaliq.com/index.htm
Tips and techniques on how to survive in the wilderness.

Note to parents and teachers
Every effort has been made by the Publishers to ensure that the web sites in this book are suitable for children, that they are of the highest educational value, and that they contain no inappropriate or offensive material. However, because of the nature of the Internet, it is impossible to guarantee that the contents of these sites will not be altered. We strongly advise that Internet access is supervised by a responsible adult.

Index